I0087408

Prayer Pearls: PRICELESS INSPIRATION

A PRAYER DEVOTIONAL

All Scripture quotations are taken from the King James Version of the Bible. *The Holy Bible. Old and New Testaments in the King James Version.* 1970.

Copyright 2015. Demetria S. Banks.   All rights Reserved. No part of this work may be reproduced or copied in any form or by any means---graphic, electronic or mechanical; including photocopying, recording, taping or use of any information retrieval system without the express written consent of the author.

DEDICATION

I would like to dedicate this prayer devotional to the many prayer warriors of our land who spend a countless number of hours fasting, supplicating, praying and interceding for people and conditions everywhere - for our leaders, our nation, our government, our communities, our schools, our families, the sick, the unsaved and many other situations. Being a prayer warrior, is a true calling. It's a noble calling. It is a powerful calling. Indeed many are called, but few are chosen. Prayer is the sincere, powerful work behind the scene that's sure to result in the success of any program, event or situation.

I would also like to dedicate this devotional to my loving husband, Walter, who unselfishly allows me to share my talents and gifts to the rest of the world; and also to my loving parents, the late Mr. Albert Springfield (1941-2005) and Mrs. Annie Springfield. Because of their unfailing love and support, I am who I am today in God.

Dr. Demetria Springfield Banks

GRATITUDE

I would like to express my sincere gratitude to: Ms. A'ndrea Leavy for her editing skills; my big sis, Shenola, and Ms. Tiffany Perry for their critiquing skills; and Evg. Deloris Chapman, Evg. Juanita Bailey, Evg. Linda Brown, Evg. Annette Kinnard and Sis. Tarsha Williams for their unfailing support, love and continual prayers.

CONTENTS

FOREWORD

Luke 18:1 says *"And he spake a parable unto them to this end, that men ought always to pray, and not to faint."* Without a doubt, your prayer life is your strength. It's your saving grace. It's the glue that will hold you together amid the adverse winds of life. That's why it is important that we pray so as to gain the listening ear of God. It is important that we know how to pray, specifically calling out areas of our needs, our world's needs, our children's needs, and the needs of others around us.

Throughout the bible, we are told how God's power is released when we pray. Proverbs 3:6 instructs us to acknowledge God in all of our ways and He shall direct our path. In Jeremiah 33:3, the Lord says, *"Call unto me, and I will answer thee, and shew thee great and mighty things, which thou knowest not.* Psalm 50:15 states, *"And call unto me in the day of trouble: I will deliver thee, and thou shalt glorify me."* In addition, Matthew 7:7-8 tells us to, *"Ask, and it shall be given you; seek, and ye shall find;*

knock and the door shall be opened unto you: For every one that asketh receivedth; and he that seeketh findeth; and to him that knocketh it shall be opened." These verses are among MANY verses of scripture in the bible about prayer and what happens when we pray! Prayer is our life line! Prayer is our everything! Without it, we would fail; our plans; our marriages, our schools, our government and so many other things would fail.

I pray that *Prayer Pearls* encourages, motivates and inspires you to reach your next level in prayer!

PEARL ONE

A CLEAN HEART

Effective prayers are those that first originate from a pure, cleansed, purged heart. *"If I regard iniquity in my heart, then the Lord will not hear me"* (Psalm 66:18). A cleansed heart is one that forgives and is forgiven knowing that when we stand praying we must forgive if we have ought against any so that our Father which is in heaven may forgive us our trespasses. However, if we do not forgive, neither will our Father which is in heaven forgive our trespasses (Mark 11:25-26).

A clean heart is one that also strives daily, moment by moment, to be like Christ - to walk like Christ, talk like Christ, live like Christ, and respond like Christ to various life situations. It is a heart that concentrates more on casting the beam out of one's own eye, than pulling the mote out of one's brother's eye (Matthew 7:3-5). It is a heart that constantly whispers this small prayer within, "*Purge me with hyssop, and I shall be clean: wash me: and I shall be whiter than snow. Create in me a clean heart, O God; and renew a right spirit within me*" (Psalm 51:7, 10).

Moment of Reflection:

_____

_____

_____

_____

_____

_____

_____

_____

_____

_____

_____

_____

_____

_____

_____

_____

PEARL TWO

FAITH

Prayers are also effective when they are offered in faith, *"But without faith it is IMPOSSIBLE to please God..."* (Hebrews 11:6). The Word of God tells us that nothing is impossible with God (Luke 1:37); that nothing is too hard for God (Jeremiah 32:17); that what He has promised, He is able to perform (Romans 4:21). As a result, we can rest assure that God has the ability to do whatever we need to have done, regardless to the situation. Our responsibility is to ask Him in faith, nothing doubting, for the man that waivers in his faith shall not receive any thing of the Lord (James 1:6-7).

Faith simply believes that what God has said is undeniably true even when everything in our circumstances stands contrary to our belief. It is to have Abraham's attitude when praying. The Bible says that Abraham *"who against hoped believed in hope"* (Romans 4:18). Certainly the individual that offers his or her prayer in faith, believing God that regardless to what the situation looks like, has been or currently is, will obtain in prayer what he or she asks from God.

If you are praying and desire your prayers to be heard, then remember this scripture today - "*Therefore I say unto you, what things soever ye desire when ye pray, BELIEVE that ye receive them, and ye shall have them,*" Mark 11:24. And remember, faith, just the size of a grain of a mustard seed, is enough faith fuel to have prayers that availeth much (Luke 17:6)! You may say, "Well Dr. Dee I know to believe God, but sometimes when things are rough my faith falters." Well at those times, my dear brother or sister, be like the man who cried out to Jesus, saying "*...Lord, I believe; help thou my unbelief*" (Mark 9:24). Our loving, heavenly Father is sure to help you and strengthen you in your area of need.

Moment of Reflection:

_____

_____

_____

PRAYER DISTRACTERS OR PRAYER BLOCKERS

If our prayers are to be effective, then we must blot out what I call "prayer distracters" or "prayer blockers." Prayer distracters or blockers are those wandering, distracting thoughts that are sure to come to our minds the moment we start to pray. They could be thoughts of our plans for that day or the week that lies ahead. Or they could be thoughts of something that happened to us the day before. They could also be troubling situations that the enemy brings to our minds to distract us. They are any thoughts, all thoughts that distract us so that we are unfocused, carelessly and mechanically mumbling out words in our prayers.

Nevertheless, if we desire to gain God's listening ear, then we must press through, casting down all thoughts that hinder us from getting to God. Second Corinthians 10:5 says "*Casting down imaginations, and every high thing that exalteth itself against the knowledge of God, bringing into captivity every thought to the obedience of Christ.*" Notice from this scripture whose responsibility it is to cast down imaginations. The responsibility is yours. If we truly want a "behind the veil experience" with God in prayer, it is imperative that we blot out prayer distracters.

Moment of Reflection:

_____

_____

_____

_____

_____

_____

_____

_____

_____

_____

_____

_____

_____

PEARL FOUR

THANKSGIVING

Philippians 4:6 states *"Be careful for nothing; but in every thing by prayer and supplication with thanksgiving let your requests be made known unto God."* This scripture clearly points out that thanksgiving is a key component of effective praying. Not only are we to tell God our requests, but we are to do so with a thankful heart - thankful for the invitation to come boldly before God's throne of grace, obtaining mercy and finding grace to help us in the time of our need (Hebrews 4:16); thankful for what God has done, is doing, and is getting ready to do; thankful that we are still blessed to be among the living; and thankful that God is able to use all things – the good and the bad for our good (Romans 8:28). Oh bless His name!

Being thankful places our focus on God instead of our problems. It helps us to focus on the many blessings God has given us rather than the gloominess of our situation. It leads us into the mighty presence of God. It is there, in His presence, that we have access to His listening ear regarding our requests.

Moment of Reflection:

_____
_____
_____
_____
_____
_____
_____
_____
_____
_____
_____
_____
_____

PEARL FIVE

WORD-BASED

Effective prayers are also prayers that are based on the word of God. 1 John 5:14-15 says, *"And this is the confidence that we have in him, that, if we ask anything according to his will he heareth us: And if we know that he hear us, whatsoever we ask, we know that we have the petitions that we desire of Him."* From this scripture we can reason that when we pray according to God's will our prayers will be heard. How do we know when we are praying according to the God's will? Well, when we pray according to God's word, we are praying according to God's will for God's will is His word, and His word is His will.

God also promises us in His word that His word will NOT return to Him void, but will accomplish that which He pleases and prosper in the thing where He sends it (Isaiah 55:11). So again, it's reasonable to expect that prayers that are based on the Word of God, which are God's promises to us, are sure to release God's wonder-working power on our behalf. Oh can we picture this - A father who promises his child a gift for having a good report card. But when the father seems slow to fulfill his promise or forgets his promise, the child then says to him "But Dad, you said......!" The father then remembering what he promised to his child knows that he is obligated to honor his word. Oh my! How much more our heavenly Father will fulfill His word to us once we remind Him of His word in prayer!

What's also important to point out here, is that if we are to base our prayers on the word of God, then we must KNOW God's word in the first place. How do we know the word of God for ourselves? We take time out from our busy schedules to read, meditate and study His word (2 Timothy 2:15). You may say, "Well Dr. Dee. It's difficult for me to find time. I'm so busy. I have a lot of responsibilities and I'm so tired once I finish that I fall straight to sleep." I say unto you, if you are waiting for the perfect time, when you're not so busy, then that time won't come. The devil will do everything in his power to make sure that that time doesn't come. Here's where you must take matters into your own hands. Set a time aside during any given day(s) to read God's word. Take your walk with the Lord serious enough to make this small investment, even if it's just 10 or 15 minutes. You will soon discover that this time will not be enough for the hunger growing inside of you for the word of God. Trust me. Your sacrifice will be well worth it!

Moment of Reflection:

_____

_____

_____

_____

_____

_____

_____

_____

_____

_____

_____

_____

_____

_____

PEARL SIX

THE SEAL

"If ye shall ask any thing <u>in my name</u>, I will do it." John 14:14

One night as I was ending *Break Away 30* intercessory prayer, the Spirit had me repeat "in the name of Jesus, in the name of Jesus," over and over. Now of course through the years, I always close out prayer "in the name of Jesus," but it was different this time. The Spirit of the Lord spoke swiftly to me, letting me know that the phrase "in the name of Jesus" was the closing seal on prayer that night, assuring us that what we had asked for in Jesus' name, God was going to do it.

Well, what had we asked for? We asked for remedies or solutions that were according to God's will for us. We asked for healing, salvation, deliverance, for God to bless leadership; to make the impossible, possible, for Him to turn situations around for our good. Since all of what we had asked for was in agreement with God's will, when we closed with the seal "in the name of Jesus," we could be assured that God heard our prayers and was going to grant us the petitions asked of Him.

Of course this doesn't mean that praying in Jesus' name is some type of "formula" we can use that will guarantee us that God will grant us whatever we ask. It simply means that we can approach God in prayer on the authority Christ has given us to use His name, and claim everything (healing, deliverance, salvation, victory, peace, etc.) that His name represents.

Moment of Reflection:

_____

_____

_____

_____

_____

_____

_____

_____

_____

_____

_____

_____

PEARL SEVEN

OBEDIENCE

John 15:7 *"If ye abide in me, and my words abide in you, ye shall ask what ye will, and it shall be done unto you."*

The word of God says to obey is better than sacrifice (1 Samuel 15:22). Throughout the Bible we are told and reminded that our blessings, our successes are linked to our obedience to God. Joshua 1:8 tells us that as we observe to do according to everything that is written in the book of the law, we will make our way prosperous and shall have good success. Deuteronomy 28:1-2 says if we hearken diligently to the voice of the Lord and do all the commandments which God has commanded us, our blessings will overtake us. Finally, 1 John 3:22 tells us that we receive from God whatsoever we ask because we keep His commandments and do those things that are pleasing in His sight.

Perhaps you may ask, "Does God really mean we can receive ANYTHING we ask as long as we keep his commandments?"

24

Well, I believe that when we abide in Christ, allowing His every word to abide in us, then we won't ask Him for anything that is contrary to His will. Our thoughts, our desires, our asking will line up with His Word. When our thoughts, desires and asking line up with God's word, then we can be assured that we will receive those things which we ask.

Moment of Reflection:

_____

_____

_____

_____

_____

_____

_____

_____

_____

_____

_____

_____

_____

_____

PEARL EIGHT

PERSEVERANCE

James 5:16(b) "...*The effectual fervent prayer of a righteous man availeth much...*"

The word perseverance, in my opinion, is to continue in a course of action regardless to whatever distractions, temptations, disappointments or discouragement that comes your way. A person who perseveres is steadfast, unmoveable, unwavering in trying to reach his or her goal.

If we desire our prayers to be effective, then we must persevere in praying – praying until the very thing we are asking God for comes to pass. Perseverance cannot be emphasized enough! Consider a child who continuingly asks his parents for a gift that they have promised him or her. Because the child continues or persist in his asking, the parents finally consent lest the child continues to worry them.

We find a similar example in the story of the widow and the unjust judge in Luke 18. The widow persisted in asking this judge to avenge her of her adversary. For a while, the unjust judge was not moved by her request. But, finally he reasoned within himself (and I'm paraphrasing), "Let me give this woman what she asks for lest she keeps coming and worry me to death."

If our prayers are to be effective, then we must persevere in our asking as did the widow in this story. Many times you will be tempted to give up; sometimes disgusted enough to give up; other times, angry enough to actually give up because it seems as if God isn't listening and if He is listening, He is not moving fast enough on your behalf. BUT, at this moment, at these moments, this is when you must "press through until you break through," until your desired request manifests. Be like the widow in Luke 18. She didn't lose heart or faith because she had asked a few times and didn't get an answer. But, she kept the faith and kept right on asking until she got her heart's desire.

Praying persistently or persevering in prayer is not unbiblical. Some may see it as a sign of weakness or unbelief. They reason that if you really believe God when you first ask, then why ask Him again and again. I believe this approach works as well.

On the other hand, I also believe in the concept of persistence in praying in faith. There are several scriptures in the Bible that illustrate this point. I have already brought your attention to two – James 5:16(b) and the story of the widow and unjust judge in Luke 18. Even before you read this story, verse 1 of Luke 18 says, *...men out always to pray, and not to faint."* Also, 1 Thessalonians 5:17 tells us to *"Pray without ceasing."* Indeed, effective prayers are prayers that are persistent in the midst of challenges, disappointments, frustrations, and discouragement!

Even the Apostle Paul said in many of his letters to the churches (for example, Philippians, Colossians, 1 Thessalonians, etc.) that he ceased not to pray for them. It wasn't because Paul didn't believe that the Lord didn't hear him when he first prayed; but, the Apostle was simply being persistent, unwavering in covering the new converts with prayer.

In contrast, I also believe that there are some who ask God over and over not because they are being persistent, but because they never really have faith in the first place that God will do what they are asking Him to do. They say things like "Well, maybe I didn't ask right. So I'll ask Him again." "Maybe, God is not going to answer me this time, because this is the same thing He helped me with last month. I shouldn't have the nerve to ask Him again." Or they reason, "Maybe, I should just stop praying. I'm not living perfectly." Notice their use of the word "maybe," which indicates that a certain amount of uncertainty exist in them already. They persistently ask God because they really do not have faith that God is going to do what they are asking Him to do. Thus being persistent in prayer, means being unshakable in one's asking, while asking in faith.

Moment of Reflection:

_____

_____

PRAYERS

PEARL NINE

PRAYER FOR MARRIAGES

Dear Lord, we thank You for this blessed union. You said in Your word that "...*What therefore God hath joined together, let no man put asunder*" (Matthew 19:6). So be it according to Your word. Lord, continue to bless, strengthen and bind us together in Your love. Help us to remember to put You first; knowing that if we acknowledge You in everything concerning this marriage, You will direct our paths (Proverbs 3:6).

Help us also to respect and value one another, being kind to one another, tenderhearted, forgiving one another, even as God for Christ sake has forgiven us (Ephesians 4:32). Let us be united and strong as a couple, praying together, studying and discussing your Word. Help us both to be better listeners and to seek to understand one another even in the midst of disagreements. Help us to lay aside weights of bitterness, anger and unforgiveness that will only serve to divide us. Yea Lord, heal our marriage of any hurt or wounds that have occurred. Help us to draw closer to You and to each other (James 4:8).

Help us also to remember that we are no longer two, but one, one flesh (Matthew 19:6a). Let each esteem other better than themselves, rising above selfishness and self-centeredness (Philippians 2:3). Truly marriage calls for both sides to give and take and many times to give up one's right to be right for the sake of peace.

Dear Lord, also help us to function in the roles Your word has prescribed for us - husband loving the wife and giving honor unto the wife as the weaker vessel (Ephesians 5:25; 1 Peter 3:7) and the wife, submitting herself to her own husband, reverencing her husband (Ephesians 5:22, 33). When marriage operates according to Your order and directives everything works for our good. Lord, we ask You for Your continual blessings, protection, healing, and favor upon this marriage. In Jesus name we pray, Amen.

PEARL TEN

PRAYER FOR A TROUBLED CHILD

Dear Lord, thank You for the child You have blessed me with. You are the giver of all life (Acts 17:28), and it is not by happenstance that You have allowed my child to be born. I thank You for this "good gift" for every good and perfect gift comes from You, with whom there is no variableness, neither shadow of turning (James 1:17).

Lord, I ask You to be with my child everywhere he/she goes. Shield and protect them from all manner of evil, giving Your angels charge over them (Psalm 91:11). Cover him/her with the precious blood of Jesus. Let no evil befall them (Psalm 91:10). Help my child to make righteous decisions. Give them to acknowledge You in all their ways knowing that You will direct their path (Proverbs 3:6). Bless them with a hunger for righteousness and the things of God for You said in Your word that blessed is he that hungers and thirsts after righteousness for they shall be filled

(Matthew 5:6). Fill them with the desire to seek after You and to forsake all evil. Give them an obedient and respectful spirit to me, as their parent, that it may be well with them (Ephesians 6:2). Bless them with the mind also to respect their elders and to submit to the laws of the land (1 Peter 2:13).

Dear Lord, I ask You to tear down strongholds and all evil influences in his/her life. Whatever area he/she is in bondage to, I come against it now in the name of Jesus, rendering it powerless over him/her. Take away their appetite for sin and unrighteousness, and give them to taste and see that You are good: blessed is the man that trusted in You (Psalm 34:8). Give them to cry out to You in the day of trouble and You will deliver them (Psalm 50:15).

I come against all generational curses that will prohibit him or her from reaching their destiny in You. Father, You have had a destiny in mind for them every since the day they were born (Jeremiah 1:5). Help them to fulfill this destiny regardless to whatever distractions or detours that exist or may come in their lives. Lord, keep them from all influence of drugs, gangs, sexual promiscuity, and crime knowing that to refrain from these things is what pleases You and will help them to walk in freedom (Proverbs 4:26-27). If they have fallen in the snare of any of these things or others, God, You are more than able to deliver them. Absolutely nothing is too hard for You (Genesis 18:14). Whom You make free, is free indeed (John 8:36).

If they are unsaved, give them the mind to want to be saved. Or, if they have turned their backs on the relationship they once had with You, stir up their hearts, minds, and spirits to return to You for You are married to the backslider (Jeremiah 3:14). Help them to not give in to any religion that does not acknowledge Jesus as Your only begotten Son (John 3:16). Of truth, there is no other name under heaven given among men, whereby we must be saved (Acts 4:12).

Bless them to be successful in all their works - their jobs, their careers, and at school, knowing that as they observe to do according to what is written in Your word,

You will make their way prosperous and bless them with good success (Joshua 1:8). When they feel that no one cares or that no one loves them, let them experience the breadth, length, depth and height of Your everlasting love (Ephesians 3:18). Help them to know who they are in You which will help build their self-esteem (1 Peter 2:9). In Jesus name, I pray Amen.

PEARL ELEVEN

PRAYER FOR HEALING

Dear Lord, it's so refreshing to know that regardless to whatever the affliction, sickness or disease may be, You are able to heal. No sickness, disease or affliction stands above Your name and at Your name all sickness must bow (Philippians 2:10). You indeed are the Balm in Gilead that heals not only the sin sick soul, but that's able to heal me (Jeremiah 8:22).

Throughout Your Word, I read where You healed ALL manner of sickness and disease, even those that were incurable (Matthew 4:23). You healed leprosy (Luke 17:11-19); a blood issue of 12 years (Matthew 9:20-22); the blind (Matthew 9:27-30), the paralyzed and the dumb (Matthew 15:30); and even brought the dead back to life (Luke 8:51-55)! With a miraculous track record like this, I can't help but believe Your word!

Your word says that healing is Your children's bread (Matthew 15:22-29). I believe this word that healing belongs to me. In spite of the pain, weakness or sickness that I feel, I stand in agreement with Your word that with Your stripes I am healed (Isaiah 53:5).

I thank You for touching my body, removing pain, taking away weakness, restoring strength, clearing up any and all infections, causing whatever is wrong to go right, destroying what needs to be destroyed, and mending what needs to be mended. Oh bless You! You are my Lord that healeth me - my Jehovah-Rapha, the Great Physician (Exodus 15:26). You are the Sun of righteousness with healing in Your wings (Malachi 4:2). Thank You, dear Lord, for restoring health unto me and healing me of all my wounds (Jeremiah 30:17). In Jesus name I pray, Amen.

PEARL TWELVE

PRAYER FOR A JOB CRISIS

Dear Lord, I trust in thee. I hope in thee. I rest in thee. Look upon the crisis situation that I am faced with on the job. Lord, my life, my job is in Your hand. Stand for my help in everything. Let every liar and worker of deceit be exposed.

You said in Your word that You will cause those that rise up against me one way, to flee before me seven ways (Deuteronomy 28:7). You also said in Your word that the wicked man conceives evil and is pregnant with mischief and gives birth to lies, but the pit he makes, he falls in it himself (Psalm 7:14-15). You told me that I should not fret because of evil doers nor be envious against the workers of iniquity, for they shall soon be cut down and wither as the green herb. That if I delight in You and do good, I shall be fed (Psalm 37:1-3).

Dear Lord, help me to trust You and do good even in the midst of this trying situation, knowing that I can overcome evil with good (Romans 12:21). Help me not to fret no matter what the situation may be, because regardless, You still are in control.

Lord, look upon my supervisor now. Even if he or she deals harshly or unfairly with me, help me to take my pain, frustration and anger and lay it at your feet, casting all my care upon You for You careth for me (1 Peter 5:7). As I need my job to help sustain me and my family, help me to pray for authority that it may be well with me (1 Timothy 2:1-2). Help me also to submit to authority, although it may hurt, even as You told Hagar to submit to Sarah when she dealt harshly with her, knowing that You had a divine plan in mind for Hagar (Genesis 16:6-9).

Father I know that the king's heart is in Your hand and as the rivers of water, You turn it whatsoever you will (Proverbs 21:1). Touch the heart of my manager or supervisor, I pray. Let me find favor in their sight. Give them to see that I mean them no harm; that I carry out my duties in a respectable and honest way, bringing glory to You, while at the same time helping the company reach its goals. I trust that if it is Your will for me to leave,

You will make it clear so that I have no doubt (Proverbs 3:5-6).

If the crisis involves a job promotion for which I was overlooked, my times are still in Your hand (Psalm 31:15). Help me to find comfort in knowing that what You have for me it is indeed for me and me alone. As You have said, "*Promotion cometh neither from the east, nor from the west, nor from the south. But God is the judge: he putteth down one, and setteth up another*" (Psalm 75:6-7). I trust that when it is time for my promotion the gates of hell will not prevail against it (Matthew 16:18).

If it's news of a soon job closure that's the source of my crisis, You are still my shepherd and I shall not want (Psalm 23:1). I firmly believe and am confident that this crisis will not prevent Your hand from supplying all my need according to your riches in glory by Christ Jesus (Philippians 4:19). If the crisis has more to do with me not performing my job effectively, help me Lord. Teach me. Guide me. Bless me with the wisdom and understanding I need to perform all my job assignments (James 1:5). I believe that I can do all things through Christ which strengthened me (Philippians 4:13). Lord, thank You for lifting the stress and unrest caused by this work crisis. Thank You for calming my nerves and blessing me with the assurance that everything will be alright. In Jesus name I pray, Amen.

PEARL THIRTEEN

PRAYER FOR A FINANCIAL CRISIS

Father, I thank You for how You have been a provider for me throughout the years and sustained me even in times of lack. You were a blessing in times of fatness and times of leanness. You proved Yourself over and over again, that You are Jehovah-Jireh, my Provider (Genesis 22:14).

And now dear Lord, look upon my financial crisis right now. Lord deliver me. Provide a way of escape for me (1 Corinthians 10:13). Send forth increase. Send now prosperity (Psalm 118:25). The earth is Yours and the fullness thereof; the world, and they that dwell therein (Psalm 24:1). Even the cattle upon a thousand hills belong to You (Psalm 50:10).

Lord, deliver me from financial lack, not for any selfish gain on my part, but so that the strain and stress it has caused be lifted from me. I also want to be a blessing to others and to the work of Your kingdom. You said that I should owe no man anything, but to love one another

(Romans 13:8). It is my desire to pay off my debtors and not live from paycheck to paycheck.

Lord, I repent of any overspending I have done and any overextension of credit I have received. I also repent of any bad habit(s) I have that has caused me to be in this financial bind (1 John 1:9). Lord, I ask You that as I continue to bring my tithes and offerings into Your storehouse, have mercy upon me and deliver me. Open up the windows of heaven and pour me out a blessing that I do not have room enough to receive (Malachi 3:10).

If I have robbed You of my tithes and offerings in order to pay bills, Lord forgive me. I believe Your Word that You shall supply all my need according to Your riches in glory by Christ Jesus (Philippians 4:19). I know that because You are my shepherd, I shall not want (Psalm 23:1) and that the little I have can become much in Your hands. Just as You took two fishes and five loaves of bread, blessed it, and fed 5,000 men not including women and children with 12 baskets left over (Matthew 14:17-21), You are able to take my little and cause it to be exceeding abundantly more than I can ask for or think according to the power that worketh in me (Ephesians 3:20).

Lord, thank You for helping me. Thank You for blessing me. Thank for delivering me. In Jesus name, I pray Amen.

PEARL FOURTEEN

PRAYER FOR THE MIND

Lord, Your word says, *"For God hath not given us the spirit of fear; but of power, and of love, and of a sound mind"* (2 Timothy 1:7). This lets me know that any and everything that is not of a sound mind is not of You neither from You. It is from the tormentor, the devil.

Lord, You have promised that as I keep my mind stayed on You, You will keep me in perfect peace (Isaiah 26:3). Forgive me if I have allowed any wayward thought, stress, strain or pressure prevent my mind from staying on You, robbing me of the peace You have promised me. Help me to gird up the loins of my mind, being sober and watchful until the end (1 Peter 1:13).

You have given me the responsibility to cast down imaginations and every high thing that exalteth itself against the knowledge of God and to bring into captivity every thought to the obedience of Christ (2 Corinthians 10:5). Help me Lord to take authority over my thought life. When the spirit of torment, torture and

46

vexation tries to take over my mind, help me to cast it down.

As Your word states, "*as a man thinketh in his heart so is he*" (Proverbs 23:7). So help me to think on things that are true, honest, just, pure, lovely and are of a good report (Philippians 4:8). Thinking on these thoughts will help me obtain your peace. Lord, also help me to renew my mind day by day, by reading, meditating and living according to Your word. It is through mind renewal I am transformed (Romans 12:2).

I also come against confusion in my mind, knowing that You are not the author of confusion but of peace (1 Corinthians 14:33). I come against double-mindedness because a double-minded man is unstable in all his ways and cannot receive from You (James 1:6-7).

Dear Lord, I thank You for bringing peace, focus and healing to my mind. I believe that before I called you, You answered, and while I was yet speaking, You heard (Isaiah 65:24). I thank You for delivering my soul in peace from the battle that was within me (Psalm 55:18). In Jesus name, I pray, Amen.

PEARL FIFTEEN

PRAYER FOR DEPRESSION

"Hear my cry, O God; attend unto my prayer. From the end of the earth will I cry unto thee, when my heart is overwhelmed: lead me to the rock that is higher than I" ((Psalm 61:1-2). Dear Lord, out of the depths of my soul I cry unto thee. Hear my voice. Let thine ears be attentive to the voice of my supplications (Psalm 130:1-2). I look to thee, to the hills from which cometh my help, knowing all my help comes from You (Psalm 121:1). I feel weary, worn and have a sadness that I cannot shake. I know with You there is rest for my weary soul (Matthew 11:28). Lord, help me to find that rest. You are the only One who can restore my soul and lead me besides the calm, still waters (Psalm 23:2-3). Let Your rod and staff comfort me during this trying time (Psalm 23:4).

Lord, I pray that whatever's the root cause of the depression that I feel, reveal it to me and deliver me from it. Regardless to how deep the feelings are or how long they have lingered, deliver me O God, for thou art indeed a strong deliver; my God, my strength in whom I will trust (Psalm 18:1). I will call upon You, who is worthy to be praised, so shall I be saved from mine enemies (Psalm 18:3) - my enemies of doubt, despair, and discouragement. I find comfort in Your word knowing that how I currently feel won't last always. Indeed weeping may endure for a night, but joy cometh in the morning for me (Psalm 30:5). I believe this and confess it. Father, I thank You for causing the joy bells to ring down in my soul again. Thank You for lifting me out of the depths of despair. Truly, thou art my glory and the lifter up of my head (Psalm 3:3). In Jesus name I pray, Amen.

PEARL SIXTEEN

PRAYER FOR LOW SELF-ESTEEM

Dear Lord, I thank You because You truly love me for me, just like I am. I am Your workmanship, created in Christ Jesus unto good works (Ephesians 2:10). I will praise You because regardless to how I see myself or feel about myself, Your word declares that I am fearfully and wonderfully made (Psalm 139:14). I am somebody because I am Your child. By faith, I am the King's kid (Galatians 3:26). It does not yet appear what I shall be: but I know that when You shall appear, I shall be like You; for I shall see You as You are (1 John 3:2).

Father, in times of doubt, insecurity, and feelings of unworthiness, help me to see myself as You see me. Help me to put off the old man including the negative way I have viewed myself, and be renewed in the spirit of my mind (Ephesians 4:22-23). Help me to rise above any inferiority complexes I have, being confident that He who hath begun a good work in me will perform it until the day of Jesus Christ (Philippians 1:6).

I truly thank You that I do not have to make myself perfect. You shall perfect that which concerneth me (Psalm 138:8). I thank You that regardless to how I feel or what others say about me several things are true: I am royalty and chosen (1 Peter 2:9). I am accepted in the beloved (Ephesians 1:6). I am victorious and triumphant (1 Corinthians 15:58; 2 Corinthians 2:14). I am a glorious work in progress (Philippians 3:12). I am more than a conqueror in all things (Romans 8:37) and can do all things through Christ which strengthens me (Philippians 4:13). Lord, I believe and receive all the wonderful things You have to say about me. I am fully confident that as I meditate daily on these things, my self-confidence will reach heights unknown. In Jesus name I pray, Amen.

PEARL SEVENTEEN

PRAYER FOR ADDICTIONS

Lord, You were anointed to preach the gospel to the poor, heal the brokenhearted, preach deliverance to the captives and recovering of sight to the blind; to set at liberty those who are bruised (Luke 4:18). I know that whom the Son shall make free, they shall be free indeed (John 8:36).

Lord, I come to You in honesty, recognizing and admitting that this addiction has gotten the best of me. It has made me captive and bruised me in so many ways. In my own self, I am powerless against this addiction, and unless You deliver me I will not be delivered.

I know that it is not your desire for me to be captive to this or any addiction. It is Your desire for me to be whole in every way. I feel like the Apostle Paul when he said that the good that he would do; he did not: but the evil that he wouldn't do, he did. Paul was so exasperated that he cried out *"O wretched man that I am! Who shall deliver me from the body of this death"* (Romans 7:19, 24)?

Lord, deliver me now as I pray. I know that in my flesh dwells no good thing (Romans 7:18) and that they that are in the flesh cannot please You (Romans 8:9). It is my sincere desire to please You. I want to walk worthy of You unto all pleasing, being fruitful in every good work and increasing in the knowledge of God (Colossians 1:10).

Dear Lord, help me as I pray. Touch me as I pray. Heal me and I shall be healed. Save me and I shall be saved: for thou art my praise (Jeremiah 17:14). I'm trusting You with all my heart (Proverbs 3:5), fully persuaded that regardless to how long I have been bound or regardless to the strength of this addiction, You are more than able to completely deliver me!

If there is any sin in my life that has opened the door for this addiction, reveal it to me that I may repent and with Your strength turn from it (Philippians 4:13). If there are any unhealed wounds or hurts in my life that has opened the door to this addiction, reveal them to me now. As you reveal them to me, heal me of any unforgiveness, hatred, bitterness, resentment or strife that has resulted from it. Wash me and I shall be clean (Psalm 51:7). Crown me with the persistence, fortitude and perseverance that I need in order to rise above this addiction. In times of temptation remind me that because I am in You I am now dead to sin, but alive unto God (Romans 6:11). Also, let me be mindful that You promised not to put more on me than I can bear, but with the very same temptation make a way of escape that I may be able to bear it (1 Corinthians 10:13).

Thank You Lord for my way of escape! Thank You for setting me completely free! Hallelujah! With Your continual help, I will be able to stand fast in the liberty wherewith You have made me free, not entangled again with the yoke of bondage (Galatians 5:1). In Jesus name I pray, Amen.

PEARL EIGHTEEN

PRAYER FOR STRESS

The psalmist said, "*In my distress I called upon the Lord, and cried unto my God: he heard my voice out of his temple, and my cry came before him, even into his ears*" (Psalm 18:6). God it is not Your will for me to be overly stressed in any kind of way. You came that I might have life and have it more abundantly (John 10:10).

Help me find relief from the stress in my life. Calm my nerves and help me to cease from worry. Restore unto me the joy of Your salvation; uphold me with Your free spirit (Psalm 51:12). Lord, I know Your word says for me to cast all my cares upon you for you careth for me (1 Peter 5:7). But, I need Your help to cast them on you and not pick them up again. I know that because I have a friend in You, I have the privilege of carrying everything to You in prayer (Philippians 4:8). Indeed, You are the God of all comfort who comforteth me in all my tribulation (2 Corinthians 1:3-4). Father I receive Your comfort now. I receive Your consolation.

If the stress is due to poor time management or me not properly prioritizing things in my life, help me to prioritize, putting You first (Matthew 6:33). Help me to also achieve proper balance in my life and schedule times for much needed rest. I can find sweet rest in You (Proverbs 3:24). Fill me with Your peace for You are the prince of Peace (Isaiah 9:6). I will not let my heart be troubled, neither will I let it be afraid for Your peace You have left with me (John 14:27). Help me to continue to look to You from whence cometh all my help, knowing all my help comes from You (Psalm 121:1). In Jesus name I pray, Amen.

PEARL NINETEEN

PRAYER FOR GRIEF

Lord, Your word says "Blessed are they that mourn for they shall be comforted" (Matthew 5:4). Look upon me now, Jesus, for I am sorrowful in heart. My spirit is grieved within me. Be near to me, Lord Jesus. Uphold me with the right hand of Your righteousness (Isaiah 41:10). I know You are my high priest who can be touched with the feeling of my infirmities; with the feeling of my hurts, my weaknesses, yet without sin. Thank You for the invitation to come boldly to Your throne of grace, that I may obtain mercy and find grace to help me in this time of need (Hebrews 4:15-16).

Dear Lord, Your word declares that You are nigh unto those of a broken heart and saveth such that be of a contrite spirit (Psalm 34:18). Be nigh unto unto me during this time of sorrow. Let Your nearness be as a balm in Gilead, healing my heartache; lifting my sorrow; easing my grief (Jeremiah 8:22). You too were a man of sorrows, acquainted with grief

(Isaiah 53:3). You know how it feels to hurt; to feel a pain in the heart that cuts to the core. But, You also know how to heal and bind up wounds (Psalm 147:3). You raise up all those that be bowed down regardless to how deep they are hurting (Psalm 145:14). Truly, earth has no sorrow that You cannot heal.

Lord, thank You for easing the hurt. Thank You for comforting me like only You can. Thank You for sending Your help in such a mighty way. I will get through this. Time will help heal my wound (Ecclesiastes 3:4). Your grace is sufficient for me during this time and Your strength is made perfect in my weakness (2 Corinthians 12:9). I receive Your healing touch right now. In Jesus name I pray, Amen.

PEARL TWENTY

PRAYER FOR LONELINESS

Lord, I thank You that You promised to never leave or forsake me (Hebrews 13:5). You also said that You would not leave me comfortless, but have sent your Holy Spirit to be with me (John 14:18). Help me to remember during times of loneliness that You are just one prayer away. That before I call on You, You will answer and while I'm yet speaking, You will hear (Isaiah 65:24).

Lord, I know I can be truthful with You. Sometimes the pains of loneliness seem unbearable. My heart aches for human companionship – someone to listen to me; who understands me; who likes me for me. At these times, Lord, be my dearest friend. Give me the strength to hold on to You; to reach out to You; looking unto You the author and finisher of my faith (Hebrews 12:2). Lead me in the paths of righteousness for Your name sake (Psalm 23:3). Lord, help me to forsake foolishness, wrong companions, and improper activities during times of loneliness. Give me to surrender to You and to love You with my whole heart, body and soul (Matthew 22:37).

When You were alone, You looked for opportunities to commune with God. Help me to use times of loneliness to fellowship with You. You said if I seek You with all of my heart I will find You (Jeremiah 29:13). Let me use this time to draw nigh unto You (James 4:8), to reach out to and serve others (Matthew 23:11), and to develop and use the gifts and talents You have given me.

Lord, I thank You for the strength You are giving me. I thank You for the help You are sending my way. I receive it and claim it. In Jesus name I pray, Amen.

PEARL TWENTY-ONE

PRAYER FOR FEAR

Father, I know that the spirit of fear is not of You or from You. Your word tells me that You have not given me the spirit of fear, but power, love and a sound mind (2 Timothy 1:7). Dear Lord, I am tired of living under the weight of fear. Fear has paralyzed me. It has robbed me of enjoying my life to the fullest. It has kept me from reaching my fullest potential in You and experiencing Your joy. Have mercy on me now, Lord. I truly desire to be delivered from all my fears, regardless of the source. You are indeed my light and my salvation so whom shall I fear? You are the strength of my life of whom shall I be afraid (Psalm 27:1)? Surely, You are my helper, so I will not fear what man can do unto me (Hebrews 13:6). Your perfect love cast out fears (1John 4:18).

Lord, help me to trust in You with all my heart, leaning not to my own understanding (Proverbs 3:5). Lack of trust brings about fear. It brings about a snare to my soul (Proverbs 29:25). I know that in trusting You my fears are released. Let Your anointing destroy the yoke of fear in my life (Isaiah 10:27). I thank You for lifting me above all my fears. Surely, You are my glory and the lifter up of my head (Psalm 3:3).

Since death and life are in the power of the tongue (Proverbs 18:21), I declare that through Your power, from this day forward, I will not let my heart be troubled neither will I let it be afraid (John 14:27). This will be my daily declaration. In Jesus name I pray, Amen.

PEARL TWENTY-TWO

PRAYER FOR SINGLES

Dear Lord, the Apostle Paul said, "...*for I have learned, in whatsoever state I am, there with to be content*" (Philippians 4:11). At this point in my life, it is Your will for me to be single, glorifying you in body and spirit (1 Corinthians 6:20). Lord, help me to find true contentment in this state, serving You to the best of my ability in all things. Help me to rise above feelings of inferiority, sadness, and despair knowing that You love me no less because I am single. In your eyesight, I am complete in You (Colossians 2:10).

When I don't feel accepted because I am single, give me to know that I am accepted and loved by You (Ephesians 1:6). In Your appointed time, if it is Your will for me, You will send the mate You have designed for me.

I take comfort in knowing that during this time in my life, You have not left me comfortless, but have sent your Holy Spirit to comfort me (John 14:18). When tensions and troublesome thoughts arise that remind me that my biological clock is ticking, that I am past the average marrying age, that there doesn't seem to be any good prospects in sight, calm me down Lord. Help me to find rest in You and wait patiently for you (Psalm 37:7). Your word says You shall renew the strength of those who wait on You; that we shall mount up with wings as eagles; run, and not be weary; walk and not faint (Isaiah 40:31). Truly, I need Your divine help to enable me to wait on Your perfect timing without being impatient.

Help me also to redeem the time, because the days are evil (Ephesians 5:16), finding my place in the body of Christ, working in it with all my might (Colossians 3:23). Let me also use this time as an opportunity to draw even closer to You, knowing that as I draw near to You, You will draw near to me (James 4:8).

Dear Lord, sustain me in times of severe testing and temptation for You are able to keep me from falling and present me faultless before the presence of Your glory with exceeding joy (Jude 1:24). Sustain me in all times of weakness, loneliness and discouragement. When I am fainthearted and have no might against the heartaches and the desire for human companionship, let me find comfort from Your word knowing that in these times You give power to the faint and to them that have no might You increase strength (Isaiah 40:29).

Also, help me to surround myself with like-minded people that will encourage me in my faith and to flee situations and people that will cause me to stumble (2 Timothy 2:22). I believe Your word that You will with every temptation make a way of escape that I may be able to bear it (1 Corinthians 10:13). Thank you for helping me. Your strength is made perfect in my weakness (2 Corinthians 12:9). I desire to be a vessel fit for Your use in every way. I will look unto You, the author and finisher of my faith, as my example of perseverance in the midst of difficulty (Hebrews 12:2). Thank You for helping me to see that being single right now is truly a blessing. In Jesus name I pray, Amen.

PEARL TWENTY-THREE

PRAYER FOR PASTORS

Your word says that You will give us pastors according to Your heart, which will feed us with knowledge and understanding (Jeremiah 3:15); shepherds who watch over our souls, as they must give an account (Hebrews 13:17). You also told us to pray for those who are in authority that we may lead a quiet and peaceable life in all godliness and honesty (1 Timothy 2:1-2). This includes our spiritual leaders, our pastors.

Lord, I ask You to bless pastors everywhere in all things. Show them what to do, when to do it and how to do it. Fill them with the knowledge of Your will in all wisdom and spiritual understanding (Colossians 1:9). Preserve their going out and coming in from this time forth and forevermore (Psalm 121:8). Stir them to continually give themselves to prayer and fasting, building up themselves on their most holy faith, praying in the Holy Ghost (Jude 20). Bless them with the ability to lead Your church righteously in all things;

with the ability to make wise decisions and choices. If they lack wisdom in any matter, let them ask of You, who giveth to all men liberally, and upbraideth not (James 1:5).

In a time of scandals and loose morality, Lord help our pastors to maintain credibility and strong morals. The enemy desires to sift pastors as wheat, causing them shame and embarrassment, but I pray that in the time of testing and temptation that their strength fail them not (Luke 22:31-32). Help them to continue to preach the unadulterated truth of Your word even if it costs them popularity with the world. Help them to stand for what You stand for and to denounce what You denounce, calling what is right, right and what is wrong, wrong. Lead them into all truth (Psalm 25:5) and in the paths of righteousness for Your name sake (Psalm 23:3).

Surround our pastors with helpers who are of honest report, full of the spirit and wisdom (Acts 6:3) that it may not bring a reproach upon his leadership. Send helpers who have his best interest at heart, a strong love for God's people, and the ability to carry out assigned duties in a spirit of excellence. Help us to uphold our pastors' arms in the heat of the battle, as Aaron and Hur upheld the arms of Moses in the heat of the battle, then was victory given (Exodus 17:12).

Continue to prosper our pastors and bless them with good health even as their souls prosper (3 John 2). Keep your loving arms around them. Shield them and their families from all danger for You are their hiding place and shall preserve them from trouble (Psalm 32:7).

Let every worker of iniquity, men of deceit, speaker of falsehoods, flattery tongue and slanderer be cut off (Psalm 12:3). I declare that no weapon that's formed against pastors shall prosper and every tongue that riseth against them in judgment You will condemn (Isaiah 54:17). Continue to stand for their help in all things and be great by their side. In Jesus name I pray, Amen.

PEARL TWENTY-FOUR

PRAYER FOR GOVERNMENT OFFICIALS

Lord, bless our government officials everywhere, in every capacity - our President, his cabinet; Congress, the House of Representatives; the Senate, kings, mayors, governors, city and county officials; local, state and national officials; rulers everywhere that it may be well with us (1 Timothy 2:1-2). Indeed, the powers that be are ordained of God (Romans 13:1) and prayers for leadership are good and acceptable in Your sight who will have all men to be saved, and come unto the knowledge of truth (1 Timothy 2:3). I pray that all of our governmental leaders make good, sound policy making decisions not based on popularity or greed, but for the common good of all people. Give them the mind to acknowledge You in every way concerning their office (Proverbs 3:6).

Your word says, *"Woe unto them that decree unrighteousness decrees, and that write grievousness that they prescribe"* (Isaiah 10:1). Dear Lord, help our government officials everywhere to pass laws that are not contrary to Your righteousness. Rebuke the anti-Christ spirit in government that desires to pass ordinances that are clearly against Your will, Your way, and Your standards. Give our governmental officials the mind to do what is right, even when right seems wrong and wrong seems right for You said in Your word *"Woe unto them that call evil good and good evil"* (Isaiah 5:20).

Lord, crown our governmental leaders with Your wisdom, for by it kings reign and rulers make laws that are just (Proverbs 8:15). Indeed, help them to govern wisely and to be faithful stewards over the offices You have blessed them with. Order their steps according to Your word (Psalm 119:133). In Jesus name I pray, Amen.

PRAYER FOR THE CHURCH

God, in a time where many attacks and much criticism is levied against the church, I take comfort in knowing that upon this rock, Your divine revelation to Peter and profession of faith in Christ by Peter, that You have built Your church and the gates of hell shall not prevail against it (Matthew 16:18). This gives me to know that regardless to how satan tries to destroy the witness, credibility and character of the church, in the end the church shall prevail! Glory!

Lord, in times like these, help the church maintain its witness for You. Let the church lay aside bickering, malice, jealousy, envy, strife, contention, status seeking, and wrath (Ephesians 4:31), anything and everything that will negatively impact its witness for You. You said in Your word that we are the salt of the earth, the light of the world; a city that is set on a hill that cannot be hid (Matthew 5:13-14). Indeed, help the church let it's light shine before men that the world may see its good works and glorify You (Matthew 5:16).

Lord, also help the church remain focused on its mission - busy about the business of the Father (Luke 2:49) - winning souls, helping the sick, healing the broken hearted, blessing the widows, visiting those in prison, ministering to the poor and needy. Of truth, You are soon to return. Don't let the church be caught with its work undone (John 9:4). In Jesus name I pray, Amen.

PRAYER FOR SALVATION

Ephesians 2:8 says "*For by grace are ye saved through faith; and that not of yourselves: it is the gift of God. Not of works lest any man should boast.*" In addition, Romans 10:9-10 says "*That if thou shalt confess with thy mouth the Lord Jesus, and shalt believe in thine heart that God hath raised him from the dead, thou shalt be saved. For with the heart man believeth unto righteousness; and with the mouth confession is made unto salvation.*"

In order to be saved one must:

1. Admit that he or she is a sinner.

2. Believe in their heart that God raised Jesus from the dead.

3. Confess Jesus as Lord. John 1:12 says "*But as many as received him, to them gave him power to become the sons of God.*"

Say this prayer: Lord, I admit that I am a sinner. I have lived contrary to You and what You represent. I ask you to forgive me and to cleanse me from all unrighteousness (1 John 1:9). I receive your forgiveness and ask You to come into my heart. I believe that Jesus Christ is Your Son; that He lived, was buried, but You raised Him up on the third day (1 Corinthians 15:4). I believe this and confess it. I receive You into my heart this very moment. Lord, thank You for coming into my heart. Teach me, lead me and guide me from this day forevermore. Lead me to a church where I can establish my membership, assemble with the saints, and grow by Your word (Hebrews 10:25). In Jesus name I pray, Amen.

PEARL TWENTY-SEVEN

PRAYER FOR THE BACKSLIDER

God, You said in Your word that You are married to the backslider (Jeremiah 3:14). Lord, I am sorry that I have turned from following You. I am sorry that I have allowed my waywardness to get the best of me. Forgive me dear Lord and restore me. Yes Lord, for Your name sake forgive my sins (Psalm 25:11).

Purge me with hyssop and I shall be clean. Wash me and I shall be whiter than snow (Psalm 51:7). Restore unto me the joy that I first experienced with You (Psalm 51:12). Lord, help me and strengthen me so that I do not fall into temptation again (Ephesians 3:16). Take away my desire for those people, things, and situations that have caused me to stumble in my walk with You. Increase my desire for more of the things of God - Your righteousness, Your truth (Matthew 5:6). Fill me more and more with Your spirit that I may live a victorious life (Ephesians 5:18).

Help me to forgive myself and to not allow unforgiveness, guilt and condemnation to weigh me down (Romans 8:1; 1 John 1:9). Help me also to reject the lies of the accuser of the brethren (Revelation 12:10) who tries to convince me that I am not forgiven, that I am still a bad person. He is a liar and the father of lies (John 8:44). As far as the east is from the west, so far have You removed my transgressions from me (Psalm 103:12). As I resist him and his lies, he shall flee from me (James 4:7). Lord, I thank You for forgiving me. I thank You for restoring me. I thank You for loving me. I thank You for receiving me again. In Jesus name I pray, Amen.

PEARL TWENTY-EIGHT

THE FAITHFUL FEW

Matthew 18:20

"For where two or three are gathered together in my name, there am I in the midst of them."

Throughout the years at our prayer time at church, the Lord blessed in miraculous ways! We saw great healings, deliverances, and breakthroughs take place before our very eyes! Oh, it was something to behold! Smiles are all over my face as I reminisce about the great times we had. God is truly a wonder; so holy; so righteous; so glorious. I could go on and on and on. But, let me get back to the point I was making.

Some days there were several people attending. Other days, especially when the weather was unfavorable, there were few. It was at one of those times, when attendance was really small, that God reminded me so profoundly that it doesn't take a room full of people in order for Him to answer prayer, for as He promised in His word that where just two or three are gathered together in His name (Matthew 18:20), He's surely there. Every since then, that scripture has truly been a blessing to me.

I never allowed the number in attendance at prayer to affect me in any manner, but particularly after God spoke to me, I get excited on days when there are few in number, knowing that with just two or three present severe damage is still done to satan's kingdom! Indeed, one can chase a thousand and two can put ten thousand to flight (Deuteronomy 32:30) Then, too, simply knowing that God is there - the One who has the ability to do whatever we need done is more than enough!

Share your thoughts.

Is the hand of God moved by the number of people present at prayer? _____

_____

_____

_____

_____

_____

_____

_____

_____

_____

_____

Should you be less eager to give prayer your all when only a few people are present? _____

Why or why not? _____

_____

_____

_____

_____

_____

_____

_____

_____

_____

_____

_____

_____

_____

PEARL TWENTY-NINE

GOD IS IN THE WEIGHTLIFTING BUSINESS

Matthew 11:28-30

"Come unto me, all ye that labour and are heavy laden, and I will give you rest. Take my yoke upon you and learn of me; for I am meek and lowly in heart: and ye shall find rest unto your souls. For my yoke is easy, and my burden is light."

One evening, I was heavily burdened after reading and receiving many prayer requests from individuals in dire need of God's intervention. I wanted God to move swiftly and provide immediate relief. The Spirit of the Lord brought sweet comfort to my soul when He spoke to me and said "God is in the weight lifting business." I tell you my soul danced within me! I could have run a couple of laps around my house, rejoicing off the Word God gave me to comfort me and tell others. Truly, it doesn't matter WHAT THE WEIGHT IS, our God is well able to lift any and every weight! Glory!

I know that sometimes the weight of our burdens distract us and cause us to doubt God and His ability to help us, but in times like these, take comfort in knowing that there is ABSOLUTELY NOTHING, GOD CAN NOT DO! Glory! Take comfort in knowing that God will never let you down! Take comfort in knowing *"that the trial of your faith, being much more precious than of gold that perisheth, though it be tried with fire, might be found unto praise and honour and glory at the appearing of Jesus Christ"* (1 Peter 1:7). Indeed! Take comfort in knowing that God knows where He is taking you, and when He gets through trying you, you shall come forth as gold (Job 23:10).

If you are experiencing a trial right now, how does the statement "God is in the Weightlifting Business" bring comfort to you?

_____

_____

_____

_____

_____

PEARL THIRTY

TIC TOC

2 Timothy 2:3

"Thou therefore endure hardness, as a good soldier of Jesus Christ."

One day in my college years, I was really going through something. I can't remember specifically what it was, but I remember it caused me to feel really down for several days. I moped around here and there, not knowing exactly what to do, not saying much of anything. My mom, with her motherly instinct, asked me what was wrong. Of course like children do, I shrugged my shoulders and replied "Nothing." But mom knew better. They always do.

As I sat sighing on the couch in our den, God spoke to me so gently and sweetly. He said "Demetria, you've got to be like the Timex watch. You've got to take a licking, but keep on ticking." Oh my! You would have thought I received a million dollars or something! Immediately, I mean IMMEDIATELY, the burden I had been carrying lifted! It was if it had never been there. Nothing like when the Master speaks to us! Just **ONE WORD** from Him makes everything alright!

Has God ever sent you a rhema word? _____ If so, how did it make you feel? Can you draw strength from it to use in a trial you are facing now?

_____

_____

_____

_____

_____

_____

_____

_____

_____

_____

_____

_____

_____

_____

_____

PEARL THIRTY-ONE

THE MUMMY LAYERS

John 11:44

"And He that was dead came forth, bound hand and foot with grave clothes: and his face was bound about with a napkin. Jesus said unto them, Loose him. And let him go."

One Saturday morning during Break Away 30 intercessory prayer, the Spirit of the Lord gave me to intercede for a woman who had called in on the prayer conference line. In the Spirit, I could see that for years this lady had been wrapped in several layers, "mummy layers." It seemed that each of the distressing things she had experienced in life represented a layer. God gave me to tell her that He was loosening her from each layer, freeing her from many years of bondage! Oh I can hear her voice like yesterday as I write. She began to cry out aloud – a cry of relief, a cry of deliverance.

So I say unto you today, if you have been bound with "grave clothes," for years and years, wrapped in layer on top of layer on top of layer, there is deliverance for you! Oh yes it is! It doesn't matter how long you've been bound or what the source of your bondage is, the Spirit of God is more than able to completely set you free!

What "mummy" layers are holding you captive?

_____

_____

_____

_____

_____

_____

_____

_____

_____

_____

_____

_____

_____

_____

How has this affected you?

_____

_____

_____

_____

_____

_____

_____

_____

_____

_____

_____

_____

_____

_____

_____

_____

_____

_____

Do **YOU** believe that God is able to deliver you? _____ If so, begin to thank God for each area (specifically call out each area) that He is delivering you from! If not, ask God to help you, to open up your understanding to who He really is and what He can do.

PRAYER POWER

Joseph M. Scriven wrote a poem in 1855 entitled, "What a Friend We Have in Jesus," in order to comfort his mother who lived far away from him. It wasn't until 1868 that a tune was composed for it by Charles C. Converse.

Even without the melody, the mere lyrics to this song are so comforting, reminding us of the power of prayer. A portion of the lyrics say:

> *"What a friend we have in Jesus. All our sins and grieves to bear. What a privilege it is to carry, everything to God in prayer... O what peace we often forfeit. O what needless pains we bear. All because we do not carry, everything to God in prayer."*

These words bring sweet peace to our hearts and souls letting us know that we do not have to worry about anything; that we do not have to carry any burden or heavy load. All we have to do is take our burdens to the Lord and leave them there with Him. O bless the Lord! We can take our burdens to God in prayer and then rest in Him because He has the ability to do whatever we need done!

Without a doubt, prayer releases the power of God in a way like no other! It releases the power of God in miraculous ways! It releases God's power in wonder-working ways! It releases His power to heal, to fix, to mend, to deliver, to break habits, to destroy yolks, to save, to restore, to strengthen, to lift, to encourage, to inspire, to change, to bless, to give life, to give direction, to revive, to resurrect, - to do any and everything we need done.

Here's a little poem that I wrote that depicts the power of prayer.

> *Prayer gives us "do right power" when we want to do wrong.*
>
> *It gives us "holding on power" when we don't want to go on.*
>
> *Prayer gives us "standing power" when we are about to faint.*
>
> *It gives us "loving power" when we want to hate.*

Prayer gives us "keeping on power" when we want to quit.

It gives us "daring power" when we don't fit.

Oh yes! My dear brother and my dear sister, prayer is power and power is to pray!

I've witnessed drug addicts and drug dealers be delivered through the power of prayer. I've seen broken marriages mended through the power of prayer. I've seen demons cast out through prayer's power. I've witnessed cancer rebuked and dried up from the roots through the power of prayer. I've seen those who were once diagnosed with terminal diseases later be given a clean bill of health through the power of prayer. I've seen high blood pressure come down, and low blood pressure come up through the power of prayer. I've witnessed life extended on those who the doctors gave only a few days to live through prayer's power. I've seen the hearts of the judge, supervisors and managers be changed through the power of prayer. I've witnessed financial doors open from out of no where through the power of prayer. I've seen God step in, in the midnight hour through the power of prayer. I've witnessed denials turned into approvals through the power of prayer. I've seen court sentences that would have resulted in at least 20 years of prison, be minimized to probation only through the power of prayer! My, my and the list goes on and on.

Prayer is truly a powerful weapon that God has given us to use in any given situation. No wonder the enemy fights us when we try to develop a strong prayer life. No wonder when it's time to pray, we get sleepier than we have ever been. No wonder when prayer is called at church, attendance is low compared to a concert or musical! The enemy knows that things happen WHEN we pray- not when we SAY 'I'm going to start praying," but when we actually start praying more. A quote from BibleGodquotes.com puts it this way, "Satan tries to limit your praying because he knows your praying will limit him." Prayer can change any condition that you have on your mind, in your heart or in your thoughts. Prayer does change things!

It availeth much for those who take the time out to pray and pray in faith.

R.A. Torrey in his book, *The Power of Prayer and the Prayer of Power*, says that:

> Prayer is the most effective work that anyone can do; that is, we can often bring more to pass by praying than we can by any other form of effort that we might put forth......We can accomplish more by time and strength put into prayer than we can by putting the same amount of time and strength into anything else. (pp. 27-28).

Sometimes we worry about many things when all we have to do is take our burdens to God and leave them with Him. Sometimes we lose too many nights of sleep because we do not take our burdens to the Lord and leave them with Him. We may take them, but then we pick them up again as if we can somehow solve them or fix them on our own. Ask yourself, "When has worrying or fretting ever solved a problem you faced?" Of course it's human nature to worry when distressing events come our way, particularly if they remain for a prolonged period of time. However, there is peace to be had when we pray about those nagging thoughts and worries that seek to drown out our faith. Without a doubt, fervent prayer will do much to calm and negate our worries. As the song I mentioned earlier says,

> *"O what peace we often forfeit. O what needless pains we bear. All because we do not carry EVERY THING to God in prayer!"*

Prayer is power and power is to pray! Do you want to be a man or woman of power? Then be a man or woman of prayer. Do you want to be a man or woman of victory? Then be a man or woman of prayer. Do you want to see deliverance and growth in your life, in your spouse's life, in the life of your children? Then be a man or woman of prayer. Do you want to see the power of God push your ministry, your program, your ideas, your organization, your business, your church, and your church leader, to heights unknown? Then be a man or woman of prayer!

If the Lord takes the time in His word to emphasize and repeat the necessity of prayer, then don't you think it is high time we become men and women of prayer? Why put off tomorrow what you can do today? Why put off tomorrow what you can begin right now, this moment? You may say, *"Dr. Dee, I have been praying. In fact I have prayed much. I have met the conditions you spelled out in effective praying; but still I'm dealing with the same thing. Nothing has really changed. I'm really tired. I don't know what else to do."* To you I say what Lashun Pace says in her song *Prayer Will Fix It For You:*

"Before you give up and let the devil win, go back and pray again!"

Through your tears, your hurts, your heartaches, your anger, your frustrations, and your disappointments, go back and pray again. You may be tired of being sick and tired, but go back and pray again!

PRAYING WITH POWER

Many times we marvel at those whom God uses mightily in prayer. Truly, God has gifted them to pray others through, to set the atmosphere for breakthroughs, healing and deliverances to occur! We are eager to hear them pray or attend a service when they are conducting prayer because we know that we are going to be blessed.

We wonder if they have some type of special "regimen" that they adhere to so that the power of God can rest upon them mightily. We wonder if they fast for weeks at a time or spend several hours each day in prayer. Surely, we reason, that there must be something special that they are doing or that God has required them to do since His power rests upon them so greatly.

Many times I have been asked if I do specific consecrations in order to prepare myself for the ministry of intercessory prayer. To that question, I honestly admit that no I do not – no special consecration, no 40 days of fasting, no praying 3-4 times a day for hours (only at times when God gives me to pray or wakes me up to pray).

I truly believe that the reason God's power to pray rest upon me in sometimes unusual ways is not because I am better than anyone else or because I spend so much time with Him, but because I keep the search light of heaven turned upon my soul, constantly asking God to search me through and through EVERY DAY, and sometimes several moments throughout the day; telling God WHEN, not if, but when You find something displeasing in Your sight, take it out because I don't want to be offensive to Him, myself or anyone else. I find myself always asking God to help me in my every area of weakness, desiring to be what He wants me to be in all things.

Indeed, I think the greatest power to be able to pray through and gain God's listening ear comes from self-examination and self-denial. Of course, we live in an age where everything but self-denial is promoted. Self is promoted in everything, even at the expense of others. I agree that self-denial can be a tough word, particularly when it calls for one to relinquish his or her right to be right; when it calls for one to humble himself or herself even when they have done no wrong. Yet, it causes the power of God to work in one's life in mighty ways, and to work on one's behalf in mighty ways.

Self-examination and self-denial begin and end with the individual. Both focus on self lining up with the word of God, on self being everything God desires it to be. Both focus on looking into the mirror, rather than pointing the finger or blame on someone else, even if that someone else is in fault. The constant prayer of both is "Lord, change me. It's not my mother, father, sister, brother, church member, co-worker, manager or classmate that is in need of prayer. But, it's me, it's me, it's me O Lord, standing in the need of prayer – in the need of Your help, Your cleansing, Your forgiveness and Your strength."

The Apostle Paul puts self examination in these words:

Examine yourselves, whether ye be in the faith; prove your own selves. Know ye not your own selves, how that Jesus Christ is in you, except ye be reprobates? 2 Corinthians 13:5

He sums up self-denial beautifully in these three words:

*I die daily.....*1 Corinthians 15:31

About DSB Life Solutions

LIVING LIFE TO THE FULLEST

JOHN 10:10

"The thief cometh not, but for to steal, and to kill, and to destroy: I am come that they might have life and have it more abundantly."

The Lord placed a burning passion in me to help His people learn to live their life to the fullest. It grieved my spirit to see so many of God's people weighed down with depression, fear, unbelief, sadness, etc. - unable to enjoy life; unable to go to their next level in God. Yes, they were Christian. Some were even filled with the Holy Ghost. Yes, they loved God; however, they were bound - desiring freedom, but bound.

Thus, "Living Life to the Fullest" (LLTF) became the premise for my life coaching business - to help, encourage and inspire others to live their life to the fullest. It is my firm belief that Jesus can and will do just what His word says - ......*heal the broken hearted; give deliverance to the captives, and recovering of sight to the blind, set at liberty them that are bruised.* (Luke 4:18). Indeed, He has born our griefs and carried all our sorrows to the cross, providing us beauty for ashes, the oil of joy for mourning, and the garment of praise for the spirit of heaviness (Isaiah 53: 4; Isaiah 61:3).

As John 10:10 states, it is the thief - the devil, our enemy, (not God, although our trials at times cause us to want to blame God for our misfortunes) – who came to take life from us, while Christ came so that we ALL can have life and have life more abundantly! Hallelujah! Isn't that refreshing to know that this promise is not reserved for some? But it's for all of us who will claim it by faith! It doesn't matter who we are; what our backgrounds are; how much money we do or do not have; or what our education levels are, with God, there is no respect of person (Romans 2:11).

As simple as it sounds, this is difficult for many to receive. They believe that the "abundant life" is for everyone except them. Satan has blinded their minds and closed their hearts from claiming John 10:10 for themselves. But I declare right now, that the devil is a liar! I come against every unrighteous seed he has planted in your mind to keep you from receiving this truth. This word is for YOU (one for the Father)! This word is for YOU (one for the Son)! This word is for YOU (one for the Holy Ghost), receive it!

So I say unto you, today, take a step in the right direction! Maybe for years you have been guilty of not enjoying your life to the fullest. Maybe for years you have allowed obstacles, wrong thinking, or people rob you of your enjoyment. Well, it is high time for YOU to take charge of your future! The prayer warrior cannot do it for you. Neither can the preacher or evangelist. You must step up to the plate. I pray that God stir you through and through to let go of anything or anyone that robs you of living your life to the fullest. May He stir you to wholeheartedly seek Him for it is there in "the seek" that you will find the abundance that you so long for.

You know, I'm a firm believer of a person having an "action plan" – something that they will put deep thought into, write down and commit to doing. Reflection is a great boost in helping us take action.

Let's take action!

What steps can you begin to take now that will help you enjoy life to the fullest? (*Remember, it takes more than writing steps down. It takes action! James 1:22 says, "But be ye doers of the word, and not hearers only, deceiving your own selves."*)

_____

_____

_____

_____

_____

_____

_____

_____

_____

_____

_____

_____

_____

_____

Perhaps it may benefit you to draw up a "contract" between you and God or between you and a person to whom you are accountable to (i.e. your spiritual mentor, church mother, a pastoral assistant, etc.) Many times when we are held accountable to do something, we are more inclined to actually do it.

Keep in mind that change doesn't come over night. If you really want change, then it will require you to be consistent, persistent, prayerful, and committed to the steps you have listed. Don't be discouraged if you do not see results right away. It is a process. Just know that remaining committed to change and God's word, as well as praying for yourself each step of the way will help yield the positive results you desire.

Also, don't be too hard on yourself if you resort back to old habits. It is our nature to stick with what we have been doing, with what we are comfortable with. Again, know that in the process of time, change will come.

Bibliography

Torrey, R.A. *The Power of Prayer and the prayer of power.* Zondervan Publishing House, Grand Rapid, Michigan, 1924.

What a Friend We Have in Jesus. n.d. In *Wikipedia*. Retrieved May 3, 2014, from http://en.m.wikipedia.org/wiki/What_a-Friend_We_Have_in_Jesus.

Other books by Dr. Demetria Springfield Banks:

25 Workplace Survival Tips for the Believer

Surviving This Place: 20 Prayers for the Workplace

Healmotions: Unwrapping the Mummy Layers

Every Single One of You: Living Above Single Life Frustrations

Between the Watch, the Work and God's Work

I Am Somebody That's Who I Am

Life Coaching Products:

Life Trac Life Coaching Series

The 3 R's of Making a Comeback

Women, Love &

Relationships MasterClass Program

To contact the author, please write:

DSB Life Solutions, LLC

P.O. Box 1877

Memphis, TN 38101

Internet address:

www.demetriasbanks.com

Email: office@demetriasbanks.com

www.ingramcontent.com/pod-product-compliance
Lightning Source LLC
Chambersburg PA
CBHW060950040426
42445CB00011B/1088